Into Science
floating
and sinking

Terry Jennings

Illustrations by David Anstey

Oxford

W

Published by Oxford University Press, Walton Street, Oxford OX2 6DP
Oxford New York Toronto
Delhi Bombay Calcutta Madras Karachi
Petaling Java Singapore Hong Kong Tokyo
Nairobi Dar es Salaam Cape Town
Melbourne Auckland

and associated companies in
Beirut Berlin Ibadan Nicosia

Oxford is a trade mark of Oxford University Press

First Published 1988
Reprinted 1990

Reading Consultant: Norman Ruel
(formerly Head of Teaching and Support Service, Reading, Berkshire).

British Library Cataloguing in Publication Data

Jennings, Terry, 1938–
Floating and sinking
1. Floating objects — For children
I. Title   II. Anstey, David
532'.2

ISBN 0-19-918257-4
ISBN 0-19-918251-5 pbk

This book was designed and produced by BLA Publishing Limited,
TR House, Christopher Road, East Grinstead, Sussex, England.

A member of the **Ling Kee Group**
LONDON·HONG KONG·TAIPEI·SINGAPORE·NEW YORK

Phototypeset in Britain by BLA Publishing/Composing Operations
Colour origination by Planway Limited
Printed and bound in Great Britain by MacLehose and Partners Ltd, Portsmouth

David collected all kinds of things.
This is a picture of them.
David filled a large bowl with water.
He put the things in the bowl one at a time.
He saw whether they would float or sink.
David made two lists like this.

Floats	Sinks
Cork	Small stone

He found that the small stone sank.
The cork floated.
Which of the other things floated?
Which of them sank?

3

Here are some things which will float.
Here are some other things which sink.
They have all been weighed.
Each heap weighs 100 grammes.
Are all the heaps the same size?
If not what differences can you see?

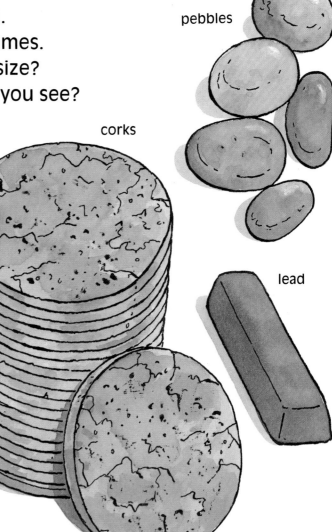

pebbles

coins

corks

lead

wood

Anna took a clean bottle top.
She put it in a bowl of water.
The bottle top floated.
Anna crushed the bottle top with a hammer.
She made the bottle top into a solid ball.
Anna put the crushed bottle top in the water.
The bottle top sank.
Why do you think it did this?

William rolled some plasticine
until it was thin.
He made a boat shape with
the plasticine.
William put the boat
in a bowl of water.
The boat floated.
William took the boat out of the water.
He rolled it into a ball.
William put the ball of plasticine into the water.
What do you think happened?
Did the ball of plasticine float or sink?

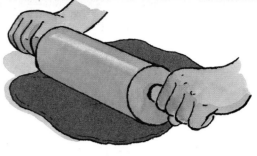

Look at this big ship.
It is taking people across the sea.
Big ships like this are very heavy.
They are made of steel.
Why do big ships float?
Would this ship float if it was
made into a ball of steel?

Caroline took an empty can.
She floated it in a bowl of water.
Caroline marked the water level on the bowl.
She marked the water level on the can.
Caroline put a disc of plasticine in the can.
The can floated deeper in the water.
The water level in the bowl was a little higher.
What made the water level change?
Caroline put lots more plasticine in the can.
What do you think happened?

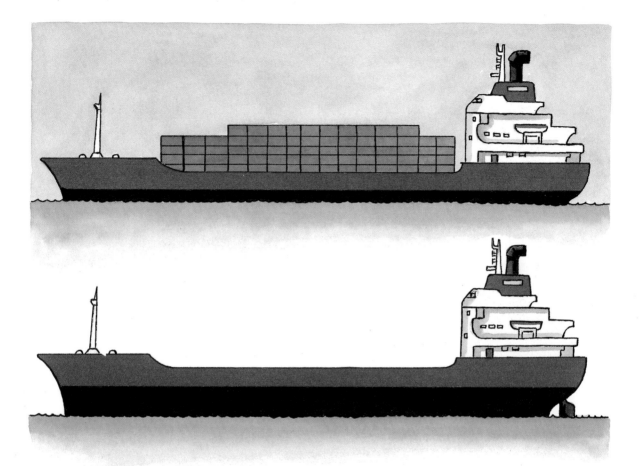

David spent a day at the seaside.
He watched a ship sailing into the harbour.
Lots of big boxes were taken off the ship.
Then the ship was empty.
This is what the ship looked like when it was empty.
What differences can you see?

Anna found four glass bottles.
They were all the same size.
Anna put water in three of the bottles.
She put the stoppers on all the bottles.
Three bottles had air in them.
One bottle had only water.
Anna carefully put the bottles in a large bowl of water.
Which of them floated?
Would the same thing have happened if Anna had used plastic bottles?

William took two empty drinks cans.
He filled one can with water.
William put the two cans in
a bowl of water.
The can which was full of water sank.
The other can floated.
William pushed this can under water.
What do you think happened?
Did the can float or sink?
Was the can really empty?

Caroline had a tennis ball.
She put it in a bucket of water.
The tennis ball floated.
Caroline pushed the tennis ball under water.
The water seemed to be pushing the ball up.
Caroline let the ball go.
It bobbed up to the surface again.
Then Caroline took a football.
She put the football in the water.
Why did she have to push much harder than she did
with the tennis ball?
Caroline let go of the football.
What do you think happened?

David had an empty plastic bottle with a stopper on it.
He put the bottle in a bowl of water.
The bottle floated.
David put a small stone in the bowl of water.
The stone sank.

David tied the stone to the plastic bottle.
The bottle held the stone up in the water.
The stone seemed to float.
What else could David have done to make the stone float?
What could he do to make a door key float?

Anna was at the swimming pool.
She wanted to learn to swim.
But she couldn't make herself float.
Anna's teacher gave her some water-wings.
The teacher blew into the water-wings.
Anna put the water-wings on.
She found it was much easier to float.
Would Anna have found it easy to float if the
water-wings had no air in them?

This is a picture of an iceberg.
It is a big lump of ice floating in the sea.
Icebergs are only found where it is very cold.
How much of the iceberg is above the water?
How much of it is below the water?
Why do you think icebergs are dangerous to ships?

A cork floats high in the water.
An iceberg floats low.
William took some blocks of wood.
They were all the same size.
William put the blocks of wood
in a bowl of water.
They all floated.
Look at the picture of the blocks of wood.
Which of them floated high?
Which of them floated low?

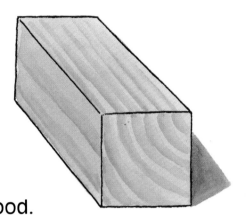

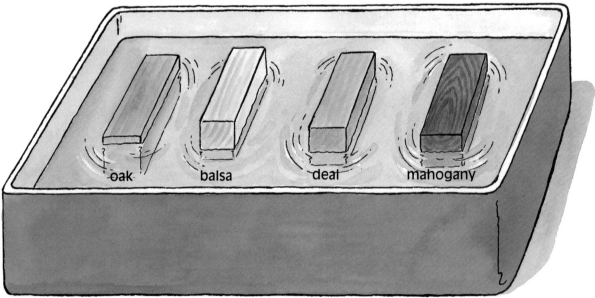

oak   balsa   deal   mahogany

Salt water helps things to float.
If something floats low in tap water, it will float higher
in salt water.
The Dead Sea is very salty.
It is the most salty sea in the world.
It is so salty that people can float easily in it.

Caroline had a block of wood.
It floated low in water from the tap.
What would happen if Caroline put
lots of salt in the water?

David made a sailing boat.
He opened a matchbox.
David put a small piece of plasticine in it.
He cut a square of paper.
David pushed the paper on to a cocktail stick.
This made a sail.
David pushed the sail into the plasticine.
Then he took an empty washing-up liquid bottle.
David put his boat on a bowl of water.
He pointed the bottle at the sail of the boat.
He squeezed the plastic bottle.
Air rushed out of the bottle.
What happened to the boat?
Before long David's boat sank.
Why did it do this?

Anna filled a jar with water.
She put a spoonful of sand in the water.
The sand sank to the bottom of the jar.
Then Anna broke up a cork into small pieces.
She put these in the jar of water.
The pieces of cork floated.
What could Anna do to get the sand and pieces of cork
back again?

22

glossary

Here are the meanings of some words which you might have met for the first time in this book.

disc: anything flat and circular in shape.

float: to stay on the surface of water or another liquid.

iceberg: a large lump of ice floating in the sea.

sink: to go down into water or another liquid.

steel: a strong metal made from iron.

water-wings: air-filled floats fixed to the arms of someone learning to swim.

index